10 easy ways to earn money from google

Deepak Yadav

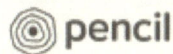

ISBN 978-93-5667-008-2
© Deepak Yadav 2022
Published in India 2022 by Pencil

A brand of
One Point Six Technologies Pvt. Ltd.
123, Building J2, Shram Seva Premises,
Wadala Truck Terminal, Wadala (E)
Mumbai 400037, Maharashtra, INDIA
E connect@thepencilapp.com
W www.thepencilapp.com

All rights reserved worldwide

No part of this publication may be reproduced, stored in or introduced into a retrieval system, or transmitted, in any form, or by any means (electronic, mechanical, photocopying, recording or otherwise), without the prior written permission of the Publisher. Any person who commits an unauthorized act in relation to this publication can be liable to criminal prosecution and civil claims for damages.

DISCLAIMER: *The opinions expressed in this book are those of the authors and do not purport to reflect the views of the Publisher.*

Author biography

I am an infopreneur and I make money online.

I learned many lessons from online learning and I want to teach this to you through my books and articles.

If you want to earn money online then you must read my books.

I hope you get to learn a lot from my books about online earning which can change your career and life forever.

CONTENTS

1. Blogger.com 12
2. Adsense 17
3. Google play store 22
4. Admob 27
5. Google Opinion Reward 32
6. Google Classroom 36
7. Google Adword 40
8. Google Task Mate 45
9. Google Map 49
10. Google Pay 52
Conclusion 54

Introduction

Do you also use all the digital mediums of today's time?

Do you know that there are many means of earning income in the internet you use?

If not, then you have reached the right place because today we are going to tell you about such a popular medium of internet in which not one but many ways are hidden to earn money.

It is a medium which is popular all over the world and which is used by every human being in the world today.

This is the site which not only earns billions itself but also provides the best means of earning to the person using it.

There are such options hidden in it, which are used by everyone, but very few people know that it is also capable of fulfilling our livelihood.

Here we are talking about the medium which will be seen in every single phone and which we need from time to time.

Having said that, without it our internet is incomplete because this medium provides us all the information as per our requirement and in this we can clear even our smallest doubts.

Now you must have understood what medium we are talking about.

We are talking about the popular medium Google.

In today's time there is no person who is not familiar with Google.

There are many people who know the importance of Google and they are using it to earn money, but very few people are not aware of the options related to it, so they are not able to take advantage of this website well.

If you are well acquainted with Google and want to know how to earn money from Google, then you have reached the right place because here today we are going to tell you about 10 easy ways to earn money from Google.

These are the methods that you can use anywhere and earn a lot of money by doing a little hard work.

Many people in this country are earning money through online and many methods are present in the internet which can give a lot of money but here you will be surprised to know that the Google which we use till date only to get information. Google has come with such options inside itself, through which we can earn a lot of money.

This is a great site for freelancing people and can earn money very easily from Google as compared to freelancing website.

Here the question must be coming in the mind of many people that how to earn money from Google?

So do not panic, here you will get the answer to your every question and all the information about all the methods that will be told here will be told to you in detail.

But before we go about those options, we should be aware of some important things related to it such as-

1. What is Google?

We all use Google but do you know what is Google after all?

So let us tell you-

Google is the largest search engine in the world, headquartered in Mountain View, California.

It is a United States multinational public company based on the Internet.

The word Google is derived from the word googol, which is a mathematical term and means 1 followed by 100 zeros.

It was founded in 1996 by Larry Page and Sergey Brin.

We can not only collect information from this multinational company, but through this we can also take advantage of internet services like advertising, cloud computing.

At present, thousands of people are working in Google's company, the services provided by it are popular all over the world and for this reason Google has become the largest search engine today.

According to a study, 3.5 billion users search on this website daily and Google has made its place among the 5 largest companies in the world.

Do you want to know how Google works and gives us the results we want?

So let us understand this as an example-

Suppose you have searched "How to make money from Google" on Google, then Google crawls the web page and sees on which pages your question is coming, which is our keyword.

Now the web page on which this question appears, Google presents it to the user and in this way we get our result.

Google indexes the web page following its rules and considering the more than 200 ranking factors present with it, indexes the web page on the first page of Google, in this way Google proves to be very beneficial for us.

2. What are the things needed to earn money from Google?

If you want to earn money from Google then it is very important for you to have all the useful things available because without it you cannot be able to earn money from Google.

So let's know what things you will need to earn money from Google-

1. To earn money from Google, it is very important to have a mobile or laptop because with the help of this you can earn money by working from home.

Without this you will not be able to use Google so these are the most useful things you need.

2. After this you need a good internet connection.

Many times it happens that due to slow network, our work remains incomplete or cannot be completed properly, so if you are thinking of earning money from Google, then you should have a good internet connection which is not possible in any way. Stay away from the network problem because if this happens you may have to face the problem.

3. The third thing you will need is the knowledge of each and every field related to Google.

Without knowledge, you cannot do any work well, so through whichever option you are thinking of earning money under Google, you should have a good knowledge of that field so that you can take advantage of every feature of that option. Best way to pick it up.

4. After all these things the most important thing is patience.

If you are thinking that any of your work will start giving you good results immediately, then it is wrong because it takes some time to start every work and it also takes time to move forward.

Earning money online is not that easy so you have to have some patience.

Think about good results and keep doing your work, this will enable you to work in the best way and you will definitely get better results.

If you have these 4 things mentioned by us, then believe me you can easily earn money through Google.

3. 10 Easy Ways To Make Money From Google:

Here now we are going to tell you what are the 10 easiest ways to earn money from Google.

This is the same option that we often use in common life and when you start knowing about them, you will be surprised how long you were deprived of these facilities.

These options have become an important part of our everyday life and without them life seems incomplete.

Just imagine how great it can be if you just take some time out and use these everyday options to make money.

So read this article carefully and think about each and every option mentioned here.

After that choose the option about which you have maximum knowledge and which you can use easily.

Once you get information about these topics then earning money from Google will not be a big deal for you and you can easily do this work anywhere.

So, without wasting any time let us come to our main topic and tell you how to earn money from Google and what steps you have to follow for this-

1. Blogger.com

You must have heard about blogging before or read in an article.

Whenever it comes to earning money sitting at home easily, the option of blogging appears first.

It is a way with the help of which we can share our daily routine, information about any subject or experience with people.

The demand for blogging has increased a lot in the internet today and there are many such websites where you can post your blogs for free and earn a lot of money.

To do blogging, you do not need much knowledge of any big technology, just you should know the art of writing as well as have basic internet knowledge related to this field.

Also, you should have grammar related knowledge of whatever language you do blogging in.

Google is a very big search engine and this is where most of the people come to get the information they want, so Google is considered to be the best option for blogging because it shows our page to the users according to the rank.

So if you can write a unique blog, then you are able to earn a lot of money through Google.

Is the question coming in your mind that what are the things you will need to do blogging in Google?

So let us tell you that to start blogging you need email id and domain.

Now everyone knows about the email ID, but the question arises that what is a domain?

So in simple words, domain is the name of a website.

That is, it is a name denoting a website, through which a blog or website is recognized.

Keep in mind that only one website can be created with the name of a domain, so the domain has to be purchased.

On social media, you will find many such websites from where you can buy domains such as godaddy, big rock etc.

If you buy a domain for a year, then you may have to pay around Rs 500.

At the same time, it is very important to keep in mind that it has an expiry date, before the end of which you have to renew it, after which you can run your website for a long time.

You will get many types of domains on these social media websites, which you will get in the form of dot com, through which you can buy domains.

After this, you will have to connect your domain to your blogger, for which you will have to use blogger.com.

This is an official website on which you have to create an account and all you need is your email id.

When your account will be created on this website, then by going to its setting option, you will see that you see the option of a domain where you have to add your domain.

After doing this much work, you will get a guideline in your screen, following which you can do further process and connect your domain with blogger.

Once your domain is connected to Blogger, after that you can start writing articles on your website.

Under this, you can choose any topic, whether it is information about a topic or a solution to a problem.

You have to take care in your written article that there should not be any kind of grammar-related mistake because it does not look good when read.

You write clearly about any topic and try to give complete information about the topic about which you are writing, by doing this the visitors visiting your website will not have to go to any other website.

Keep in mind that never copy any article and put it on your website because by doing this your article will not rank on Google nor will it be presented in front of people and you will not be able to earn money.

You have to write this type of article which is different from every article, it is unique and people like it as much as possible.

If you are writing a solution to a problem, then define every point related to it well because such articles are easily ranked on Google and visitors start coming to your website.

As soon as traffic starts coming to your website, you can earn a lot of money using your website.

You can use this website in your option like affiliate marketing, from where there are chances of earning maximum.

As you know that how much affiliate marketing has become a part of digital marketing today, so you can share their affiliate link on your website for the promotion of any brand or product and as many people can share this product through this link. The more you buy, the more you will earn.

For example, suppose you have written an article on a blog about a product like Amazon and Flipkart and together you have shared their affiliate link for its promotion.

Now when the visitors will read your block and click on that link and buy the goods, then the company of Amazon and Flipkart will give you their commission.

In this way you can earn money using your website.

You can make your website a source of advertising for people. Because today's era is of advertisements, so by bringing more and more traffic, you can do promotion work for people in your website, so that you get good money.

So in this way you can earn money from Google using blogger.com.

2. Adsense

Today's era is the era of advertising, you all know this very well.

Whether it is a small shop or a big multinational company, everyone resorts to advertising to make their product popular.

You must have often seen posters related to the product's AIDS in front of the shops on the way, this is also a means of advertising which attracts people towards the brand or product.

On the other hand, if we talk about online options, then here too you will get to see advertisements.

From television to mobile, money is earned everywhere through these advertisements.

At the same time, our Google is also not lagging behind in earning money from advertisements, in this also you will find many options to earn money through advertisements which are very popular and safe too.

One of these ways is Adsense, which is a way to earn money by showing ads with online content and it is absolutely free.

Today we are going to tell you about this method.

Adsense is a very good way for an online publisher to earn money because it pays you money according to the content and traffic coming to the website.

If you have a website in which a good number of visitors come daily, then you can use Google Adsense to show ads of any product or brand on your website.

In this program you can show those ads that Google Ads will give.

If you get good response from people, then you get paid accordingly.

This question must be coming in the mind of many people that can we show ads of our choice on our website?

So it is not that only those ads will be seen in your website, which will be approved by Adsense, that is, which will be related to your content.

Now it comes to the basis on which Google gives you money for this?

So let us tell you that you are paid according to the clicks, impressions and other interactions on Google Ads.

That is, suppose a visitor has come to your website and is getting to see an ad, then if that visitor clicks on that ad, then you get paid for that click.

Let us now tell you about it in a little more detail, how it works and how you get money from it, so that you will understand easily.

There are 2 ways to earn money from Google Adsense, one is blogging and the other is YouTube which is very popular.

Money can be easily earned using both these platforms, although the use of aids is different on both the platforms.

If you talk about YouTube, then if you have a YouTube channel and you want to get it approved with Google Adsense, then for that you have to consider some conditions like your channel should have 1000 subscribers and 4000 watch horses.

After which you can apply for monetization and if Google Adsense has approved your channel, then you can earn a lot of money by placing Google Adsense ad in the middle of your video.

Now when it comes to the website, the process is different.

First of all, you have to prepare your website and submit it to Google Adsense, after which your website is checked by Google Adsense and if your website is eligible for approval only then you get approval.

After getting the approval, you can do your work by putting ads in it, although for this you have to write good content only then you can work for a long time.

The more people who see your ad, the more profit you will get.

Suppose if you are writing a blog related to a website such as Amazon, then ads related to the same will be shown on your website and when it will benefit Amazon then you will also get commission.

Now you must have understood that how you can earn money using Google Adsense.

You have to choose a better website for yourself in which you can do blogging and secondly you have to make good videos for your YouTube channel so that more and more people are attracted towards your channel.

Once you start providing good, content and people start liking your content, then they will definitely see this ad only and only to read your content, so try to write something unique and special and on maximum good topic. Create content or videos.

The important thing to note is that you have to create content according to the needs of the people.

Because many times it happens that people come to your website or your channel to see or read the work done by you, but as soon as they see an ad, they leave that video or content and go ahead, which will benefit you. does not happen.

Therefore, prepare such a material in which people are interested, only then you will be able to get maximum benefit.

Very good money can be earned in both these ways.

3. Google play store

Google Play Store is one such application which is a must have in every smartphone and in today's era there will not be any person who would not have known or used Google Play Store.

In the Google Play Store, you will find thousands of applications, whether it is related to a game or education.

This is an application that provides applications related to every subject and from here most of the people download their desired application.

But do you know that you can also earn a lot of money using Google Playstore?

If not then you have reached the right place because here we are going to teach you how to use Google Playstore properly from which you can earn a lot.

Google Play Store is an application designed for Android users, through which users using Android can easily download any application.

You must know that every application found in the Play Store is made by an app developer, through which they earn a lot of money and you can also earn money from Google Play Store by adopting the same method. For you the most important thing should be coding.

There are two main ways to earn money from Google Play Store, one is by creating and publishing an application on the Google Play Store and secondly downloading an application and working on it.

So let's first know how we can earn money by publishing our made app on Google Play Store-

If you want to earn money by publishing an app on Google Play Store, then for this you should come to the work of app development and if you can not do the work of app developing then you can also do this work by hiring an app developer.

Suppose you are an app developer, then you can prepare such an application and publish it on Google Play Store, which people need more.

Whenever someone downloads the application that you have created, then you will get money from it, so this method is most popular to earn money.

If you are not an app developer, you can hire an app developer to do this work, although you will have to pay them something for this.

You can ask an app developer to create the app you want and when your application is ready, you can publish it on

Google Play Store.

You have to create an application which is beneficial for the people so that you can publish these apps as paid apps also.

Simply put, whenever someone downloads the application created by you and wants to use it, then he will have to pay.

If your application is good then people will not hesitate to pay for it, but keep one thing in mind that no one should publish such application as a paid app which is already available on Google Play Store for free because such If you do, no one will use your application.

Do you want to know what items are needed to make apps?

To create a good application, you should be creative so that you can make the application according to the convenience of the people.

You have to create an application that is different from other applications, only then people will be more interested in your application.

Apart from this, you should also have knowledge of coding because without this you cannot do app development work and for this you will have to invest and hire an app developer.

Now you must be thinking that how can we publish our application?

So for this you have to follow all the given steps-

1. First of all you have to create your account in Google play console in which you will need your email id.

2. After this you have to invest $ 25 only once to publish your first app and after that you can publish as many apps as you want.

3. After this you get the option of publish your first Apk on the home page from where you can publish your app.

To earn more from your app, you can promote it and for this use social media such as Facebook, Instagram and Twitter.

You can not find a better way to earn money from Google Play Store because

Here if you want, you can earn money by making an app related to any of your work and working on it.

Now we know how to earn money by downloading the app from Google Play Store-

You must have heard about many such applications or have seen their add-ons which pays for working for them such as Meesho App, Cash Karo App etc.

This is the application where you can easily earn 15 thousand to 20 thousand rupees by working a few hours.

For example we can take Meesho app.

This is a website that deals with fashion products.

Here you have to help them to increase the sales of their products, in return for which you get commission.

Suppose you have joined Meesho's company and you want to sell the T-shirts there, then you will sell it by adding your commission to its fixed rate and if you have sold more number of T-shirts then you will get commission according to its number. .

In this way you can also earn money by working for the app.

4. Admob

Who is not aware of smartphone in today's time.

Today it has become an important part of life and all the things used in it like websites and apps are also proving useful for us in many ways.

Have you ever seen ads popping up in downloaded apps?

Have you not wondered why these ads are shown and what is the benefit to anyone?

The answer is that the owner of the apps earns money by showing these ads and if you want, you can earn money by adopting this method.

The company from which these ads are shown is that of Google Admob, which is part of Google itself and can be used for Android and iOS platform apps.

Google Admob also works like Google Adsense and it earns money in the same way as in Adsense, but the difference is that Adsense shows ads for any content and Google Admob shows ads in the application.

You can easily earn money by creating an application and showing ads in it because here the more your application attracts people towards you, the more profit you will get and your earning will be.

So let us tell you in detail how you can earn money using Admob-

Admob is an advertising based company which was developed by Google itself and it is very beneficial for Android mobile and ios system because Admob's ad can be shown in these mobiles.

This is a very good resource because its size can be set according to the screen size of the users phone.

This can become a very good source of earning money for you because in today's world the number of people using apps is in crores.

Now it comes to how money can be earned through this and what things do we need?

To earn money from Admob, you will have to work a little hard and you will have to follow all the steps given here carefully after which all your work will become easy-

1. First of all you have to create Google Admob account which is very easy.

In this, you have the advantage that you do not have to wait for approval like Google Adsense, so your work becomes easier.

To create an Admob account, you must have an email id and mobile number, after that you can open its website and login to Gmail ID and create your account.

2. After this you have to fill your mobile number and address along with it.

3. After doing this, your Admob account will be created and when you open your account, some conditions will come in front of you, after accepting which a window will open in front of you in which you will have to connect with the app monetization service.

Many options will come in front of you which you will have to fire, after that you can proceed further by clicking on Continue to Admob.

Do you want to know how we can monetize our application with Admob account?

So let us tell you that to monetize any application in Admob's account, the first thing we have to do is add unit-iD generate which is available to us on our Admob account only.

When we generate our Add unit ID, we have to install it on our mobile app and after doing this our app will be monetized.

To make the work easier, you will find many platforms on social media where you can easily create android.app.

There are many platforms where we can create our own application without coding, although it is more beneficial for those who know coding.

You will find many apps like Appy builder, makerroid, thunkable where you can sign up and create your own application.

Admobe is the way by which you can earn money sitting at home by placing ads in your application.

There are many people who are earning crores through this.

Now you must be thinking that how do you get money from this?

Whatever ad audience will see in your app and click on Admob, then you will get paid for it.

To earn more and more money, you have to make your apps reach as many people as possible and make a creative application that will attract the interest of the people and only then you will be able to earn a lot of money.

You can also publish your apps on Google Play Store because you will find many users here.

In this way Google Admob gives you this opportunity that you can easily earn money sitting at home by just creating your account and publishing the app.

Nowadays the era of advertisements is going on, so if you make a creative and attractive application then you will get maximum benefit.

Here you also came to know that if you do not know coding and you want to make your application, then which website can you use to create an application without coding.

If you do not like this method also then you can hire an app developer, just for this you will have to invest i.e. the app developer will have to pay.

Keep in mind that you have to follow all the conditions of admob properly because violating them may also result in loss.

5. Google Opinion Reward

If we talk about earning money easily without cost, then here you also get the option of Google Opinion Rewards which is very easy.

This is an application where you can earn a lot of money by working and in this you only have to answer some simple surveys for which you get paid.

So let's first go to what is Google Opinion Rewards?

Google Opinion Rewards is an application from Google which is based on survey in which the user has to answer some questions after which they are rewarded.

Simply put, it is a Google money making app in which you can sign up with your email id and earn money by answering simple questions.

Here you will get unlimited surveys, answering which can earn money.

This app has also become very popular because earlier it could only be used by Android users but now it can be used in both Android and iPhone devices and has become so popular that today it has 50+ on Google Play Store. It has more than a million downloaders and its rating is also very good.

This application can be easily downloaded from Google Play Store.

Now it comes to how to create an account in this application, then this task is very easy, just follow the steps given below-

1. After downloading the Google Opinion Rewards app, open it and click on Get Started.

2. After this, you will get the option to enter Gmail ID, which you can sign up by entering.

3. Then a Google Opinion Rewards home page will open in front of you where you will have to create your profile by clicking on the profile icon, for which you will have to enter some basic information such as country, pin code, age, gender and language.

4. After filling these basic information click on complete.

Now you can see that your Google Opinion Rewards account has been created where you can earn money by answering some simple questions.

After creating an account, whenever there is any survey in Google Opinion Rewards, its notification will come to you, after which you will have to answer some questions and in return you will get money from Google in the form of rewards.

If you are wondering how to withdraw these money, then the thing to note here is that you cannot transfer the money received from Google Opinion Rewards to your bank account, rather you can use it from playstore through the tree application, You can buy movies, TV shows or e-books.

You will see your earned money on the home page of this and further you will also get the option of Play Store, by clicking on which you can use these money.

These rewards are also easy to use and it becomes even more easy for the Android user, but the new users can also use it easily by taking a little knowledge.

Here you can change your basic information whenever you want to delete the account created on it, then you can delete it.

If you want to participate in as many surveys as possible, then keep your location on so that wherever you go, you can get surveys based on location.

As you keep giving the right answers, you will get unlimited surveys in front of you.

Keep in mind that the rewards received in this also have an expiry date and you have to use them before that date ends.

That's why you keep checking its expiry date from time to time.

So in this way you can also earn money by using Google Opinion Rewards

6. Google Classroom

Nowadays education is being promoted a lot.

Many such policies are also coming out which are working to develop and encourage education.

Nowadays every parent is also trying to give better education to their children, in such a situation, if you make education your career option then you can take good advantage.

As the technological capability is increasing, the desire to learn new things is also increasing and due to this the importance of online education has also increased a lot.

Especially since the time a dangerous virus like Kovid-19 started spreading in our country, at that time all the students were sitting at home and taking online education.

Apart from this, people of schools, colleges or any other field have started giving more importance to online education.

Today's technology has also provided this facility that the teacher can give the same education to the student as in the school sitting at home and making this its medium,

Google also took a step and created Google Classroom which is online education. based on.

Google Classroom is a platform that can be used to provide education to the people.

This software is very beneficial for those teachers and students who want to exchange education for free and are unable to go to school due to any reason.

It has all the features that a teacher needs so that he can easily build a class room.

If you think that you have this art in you that you can educate people, then you can earn a lot of money using Google Classroom, it does not require much effort, you only need to have the right knowledge of the related subject and You should have this ability to explain to people.

Under this, you will find Google Calendar, Class Work Section, Grading Interface etc. which has made this platform more effective and it is very easy to use.

It works on a code that can be used to connect to each other, if you are a teacher then you have to add your student to the classroom and if you are a student then you will get the code from your teacher and google classroom You have to join by entering, but for that you have to create your account in Google Classroom.

This is a free platform that does not require any investment to use, for this you only need a mobile or laptop with a good internet connection.

Its biggest advantage is that along with the best features, it also saves your time.

Now we tell you how you can create your account on this platform-

1. To earn money from Google Classroom, you have to create an account in it, for which you must have a Gmail account and you must also remember its password.

2. You can create your account in Google Classroom in two ways, first way is to download this application from Google Play Store and login with your ID to create your account and second way is to create your account directly in Google Classroom Go to the room's website and login with your Gmail ID.

Both the methods are very easy.

3. After this you have to create class on your account for which you have to login in this account.

4. Then you will see the option of plus on the home page, on which you have to click and after clicking on it, you will see the option of create class.

5. As soon as you click on the option of Create Class, you will come across some term and condition which you have

to accept and after that you will have to fill some basic information like class name, section, subject and room.

6. After this you have to click on the Create button and you will see that your classroom has been created.

You can share its code with your students and they can join. You can also live chat with your students, making the exchange of education even easier.

In this way, you can earn a good amount of money by adopting your teaching skills using Google Classroom.

This is a great way to earn online because neither much investment nor hard work is involved in it.

All you have to do is sit in one place and educate people with your teaching skills.

Just keep in mind that whatever subject you are telling the student about, you have complete information about that subject and there should not be any kind of doubt in your student's mind.

7. Google Adword

Now we tell you about another great platform of Google, Google AdWord, through which you can earn good money in less effort.

Whenever we visit any video or website, we start seeing advertisements and through these advertisements people earn up to lakhs of rupees.

One way to earn money from these ads is Google Adword.

Google Adword is an online paid advertising program through which people work to bring their products and services to the audience.

Under this you will get all the facilities that are needed to create an ad.

Now you will think that we have already told you about AIDS, then why is another Google Ad option being told now?

But the difference here is that this program is based on PPC i.e. Pay Per Click, that means whenever a visitor comes to your website or block and clicks on your ad, then you will get money.

This program is based on two networks first is search network where you will see ads i.e. when you advertise your product on this network it will show in search result and second is display network which is more than 2 million websites and videos. There is a group of ads where ads appear which is based on videos and includes re-marketing as well as banner ads.

As you know that Google is a very big platform, so visitors are also very high here, so if you are choosing any medium related to Google to earn money, then the possibility of better results in it increases.

This program is used by the businessmen for the promotion of their product, who make their product reach the audience by making a target, it does not matter whether your business is big or small so this is a great feature.

Apart from this, even if you are a YouTuber, you can use this platform to make your content reach as many people as possible and earn money.

Google Adword is a huge platform in the world of advertising, which works to bring your product or brand to the people, so earning money from it is also very easy.

In this you can easily run your created ad in which you can also work based on your location.

You can work in it according to your budget and can also set a limit.

Using this, the work of making people aware of the brand or product can be done.

If you want to bring traffic to your website, then Google AdWords is capable of bringing traffic to your website.

The more people who come to your website and click on your ad, the more money you will be able to earn.

If you use video campaigns on YouTube, then you can show video ads on your YouTube channel, which can be very beneficial.

Using this feature is also very easy, in which you have to create your account and select New Campaign.

In this, you will determine all the things that are necessary for your campaign such as sales, leads, traffic etc.

Here you can also select your campaign type so that your ad can reach as many people as possible and after that you have to choose the network whether you want your ads to run on the basic of the search network or on the basic of the display network.

Now if you want, you can also choose the language here and you can also set the budget.

The most important thing here is the keywords because on the basis of these Google ranks your page and shows it.

Also, you have to pay special attention to headlines and description etc.

After this the last option that you get is Payment Info i.e. you can choose how you want to receive payment.

The system on which Google AdWord works is the competition on the ad pattern i.e. who is setting the big bid.

Keeping these things in mind, it works, that is, the one who will pay for more and more ads and whose quality of ads is better, the same ads will be more shows and they will get money according to the click.

For this, you have to set a good budget according to the day, the bigger the amount, the better rank your ad will get.

In this competition, whichever advertiser presents his ads in the right way by adopting all the conditions, they are shown first.

As we told you that keywords are most important in Google Adword, so if you choose the right keywords using tools like Google Keyword Planner then you will get good results.

Therefore, never use negative keywords because by doing this the service of your product will reach even those people who are not interested in seeing your adds and the budget you have set on the click will be wasted.

For example, suppose you are running a campaign in which you have not used the negative keyword, then it means that you are telling Google Ads that your ads should not appear where your audience is not targeted.

Also, keep in mind that never enter any wrong information because even these mistakes do not give us better results.

In this way, the more amount you set, the more your adds will be shown in front of the people, which depends on your audience target and when people click on your ad, you will get money according to your budget.

8. Google Task Mate

You must have heard about Google Task Mate.

This is an app that has been launched by Google itself, under which you can earn money by completing any task.

This is an early access app which is run by google access by referral code, here you will get many tasks which you have to complete on time.

You can also refer it to your friends and relatives but keep in mind that no person can refer Google Task Mate app more than 3 times in a day.

This app will be easily available to you in Google Play Store and because it is an application of Google itself, it is absolutely safe.

If you want to earn money through this, then you have to first create your account, for which you have to follow the following process-

1. First of all go to Google Tasks app and login email id.

2. After this you can select your language and if you have any referral code then you have to enter that code.

3. After this you will get the terms and conditions which you have to accept.

Here you also have to keep your location on.

4. After this you will be asked two questions which will be about GST and language. You can choose the language of your choice.

5. After this a total of 20 questions will come in front of you, which you will have to answer and when you complete this task, your account will be created.

Now comes the question, how do you get money in this?

So every day you have to answer 20 questions in Google Task Mate application, if you complete it on time then you will be given money in local currency.

Keep in mind that to earn money from Google Task Mate, you must have a good internet connection because questions are asked on the basic of the image and 20 images will appear in 20 questions, which is very important to download on time because if your If the internet is running slow then the task will not be able to be completed on time.

Whenever new tasks will come on this application, you will get notification.

Apart from this, you can also use setting task and field task.

In the setting task, you can complete the task based on your location, which will be based on the voice task.

Field task is a bit difficult to do because for this you have to work outside the house.

You have to go to the market and Google can give you any task here.

You will find many types of tasks in this, such as the task of taking a photo of an object or the task of taking a photo of a shop, etc.

When you drag and upload it, after that you may get more tasks.

Apart from these, you can also earn money by referring Google Task Mate app, but this application cannot be referred more than 3 times in a day because if you do this then your account may be locked.

If you want, you can also transfer the money earned from this to your bank account, but the condition for this is that there should be 10 dollars in the wallet of Google Task Mate app because you will not be able to transfer your money in the bank for less than that. .

Now you must be thinking that what would be the benefit to Google, then Google is able to gather more information about the local area with the Google Task Mate app, so it gives such tasks to the people.

In this way you can earn a lot of money by using this application by completing small task time.

9. Google Map

You must have used Google Map to know your location but very few people know that you can earn money online through Google Map.

Google Map is a service of Google company that gives detailed information about each geographical area to the people, here you can find the exact location and learn about new places.

By creating an account in Google Map, you can earn a lot of money from this, for which you will need an email ID.

Create your account with whatever email id is saved in your mobile and whose password you know.

Now we tell you which options you will get to earn money from Google Map-

The first option is to earn money by becoming a local guide.

In this option of Google Map, you get points, by becoming a local guide on this app, you can get many rewards which you can use whenever you want.

To become a local guide, first you have to login your email id in Google Map and create your profile.

In the profile, you will get the option of an image in which you will have to join by going to the option of Join Local Guide.

Here you have to select your location and accept some conditions, after that you can get points by becoming a local guide on Google Map.

Whenever you go anywhere, whether it is a place like a hotel, mall or shop, by going there you can give them a rating and write something about them that earns you points.

You can add options like review, rating, new place, new road inside it and you can easily redeem the points you get after doing these tasks.

Another way is to add business.

That is, if you know how to list in Google My Business, then earning money from Google Maps can be easy for you.

You can list the address of any organization, person or company on Google Map, in return for which you get money from the person who got the list and you can earn good money.

If you want, you can also promote your business through this application, so that your product will reach more and more people.

Suppose if you are also taking 100 rupees from a person to list their business on Google Map and if you get the business of 10 people listed in 1 day then you can earn thousand rupees a day.

To add a business, you will not have to work hard, just go to your profile and click on Add Your Business, after which you will have to enter the name and category of the business and fill some information related to it such as location, area, contact details etc. .

After doing this, you will get a PIN which you will have to add in Google Map, after which your business will be added to Google Map.

So these were the ways to earn money from Google Map, which can earn a lot.

10. Google Pay

In today's world, the work of online transactions has also increased a lot and people are now more dependent on online payment instead of cash.

The same online payment option is Google Pay, which is a secure medium of Google itself, from which money can also be earned.

Here's the easiest way to refer and earn.

You can share this link to your friends and relatives and whenever your friends download google pay through google pay link shared by you, you will get some commission in return.

You will be surprised to know that the most important thing in Google Pay is that if you do a transaction of 500 or more rupees once a week, then you also get a chance to win money.

If you want, you can earn money by paying bills every month with Google Pay because Google gives us the option that we can pay bills like electricity bill, TV or mobile recharge and water bill, in return we get some cashback. And get good money too.

In this way Google Pay is also a good source of earning money.

If you talk about its lucky weekend, then it chooses Lucky Friday quest card every week on Friday in which the lucky winner can also get a chance to win 1 lakh rupees.

Conclusion

Google has become a huge part of the Internet today and it is used in every corner of the world, so we get the option to earn more and more money by using it.

This world of advertising and information is a great way for people to achieve success which is very easy to use.

In all the options mentioned by us, you only need basic knowledge, after which you can take advantage of every feature.

Very few people know that a lot of money can be earned by using all the services of Google, which has become common for those who know about it.

Here you came to know about those options which we often use in our daily life but very few people know how to use them properly.

You must be surprised to know that Google, which till date was used only to get information, has so many ways to earn income.

Today's digital age has progressed so much that wherever you can see the option of income will be available, you just need to recognize it.

Here you have seen how we can make a lot of profit by using the given options.

No one can imagine that there are so many ways to earn money in these options because people do not have the right perspective to look at these mediums.

You have come to know that how the services of Google are useful for us and here we can earn money by doing whatever we want.

The thing to keep in mind is that in many Google services, you get payment on a fixed date, which comes directly to your bank account, although you can also get money through cheque.

Here you also get a chance to use your skills, so that your skills shine even more and come in front of people.

Google is a great and secure site which is different from other sites and is capable of giving you better results.

The services of Google, about which you have been given information, are absolutely free and also very popular, due to which we get the option that if we want to start any work without costing, then we can do it easily.

Many people have started their career by using these services and many people want to get information about it and start their business.

You will also find many such people who started their work with very little hard work and have reached a high level with their skills and there are many such people who have earned a good name by working hard.

Here your success depends on your work and dedication, so it may be that you can easily settle your feet in it or it may also take you a long time but if you keep working hard then one day you will definitely achieve success.

We hope that you must have liked this post of ours today and you must have got the answer to all your questions.

We have tried our best to give you every information related to how to earn money from Google and have also tried to make it easy for you to understand about every topic.

Hope today's post will give you new options and inspire you to move forward.

Please write a review about this book.

www.ingramcontent.com/pod-product-compliance
Lightning Source LLC
LaVergne TN
LVHW041636070526
838199LV00052B/3401